# Dubious Breath

*poems by*

# Jennifer Davis Michael

*Finishing Line Press*
Georgetown, Kentucky

# Dubious Breath

Copyright © 2022 by Jennifer Davis Michael
ISBN 978-1-64662-889-6 First Edition
All rights reserved under International and Pan-American Copyright Conventions. No part of this book may be reproduced in any manner whatsoever without written permission from the publisher, except in the case of brief quotations embodied in critical articles and reviews.

## ACKNOWLEDGMENTS

*Amethyst Review* ("And Then")
*NELLE* ("Physical")
*Oxford Poetry* ("And In Those Last Days")
*Poets Reading the News* ("Expectation")
*Waxing and Waning: Tennessee Tempest Edition* ("Annunciation, March 2020" and "Between Waves of the Pandemic," published as "Between Bands")

"Forty Trochees" won the Frost Farm Prize in Metrical Poetry in 2020, judged by Rachel Hadas.

"You Have No Bucket," under the title "Thirst," was part of an online service for Good Friday, 2021, hosted by St. Luke's Church, Evanston, Illinois.

I'm tremendously grateful to all who offered suggestions and encouragement as I worked on these poems: Leigh Anne Couch, Virginia Craighill, Pauletta Hansel, Jessica Jacobs, David and Luann Landon, Alfred Nicol, and Jim Pappas. While I gladly share any merits, the frailties are mine alone.

Publisher: Leah Huete de Maines
Editor: Christen Kincaid
Cover Art: *Light As* by Robley M. Hood
Author Photo: Robert Butler
Cover Design: Elizabeth Maines McCleavy

Order online: www.finishinglinepress.com
also available on amazon.com

Author inquiries and mail orders:
Finishing Line Press
PO Box 1626
Georgetown, Kentucky 40324
USA

# Table of Contents

And in Those Last Days ................................................................. 1

Expectation ................................................................................... 2

Augury .......................................................................................... 3

Annunciation, March 2020 ........................................................... 4

Enchantment ................................................................................. 5

Construction in the Neighborhood ............................................... 6

Pandemic Questionnaire ............................................................... 7

Fog Made of Stone ........................................................................ 8

Laying Out My Son's Clothes ....................................................... 9

After a Dream of the End of Spring ............................................ 10

Between Waves of the Pandemic ................................................. 11

Why I Am Not Writing a Poem .................................................. 12

Gated Community ....................................................................... 13

Dead Air ...................................................................................... 14

Forty Trochees ............................................................................. 15

Physical ....................................................................................... 16

Patient Belonging Bag ................................................................. 17

You Have No Bucket ................................................................... 18

Pentecost ..................................................................................... 19

Savanna ....................................................................................... 20

And Then .................................................................................... 21

**And in Those Last Days**

The sky was brilliant blue, implausible,
as on a postcard from a former time.
Trees shuffled all the paint-store chips of green.
Even the clouds less cloudy, more concrete.
And all of it delineated so
sharply, as when the oculist holds up
a lens a smidge too strong, and asks
if one or two's the view that you prefer.
Seduced by clarity, you opt for one,
but later long, with aching eyes, for the blur.

This was the sharpness just before the end:
light shimmering as if brushed on by Vermeer,
the paint about to crack under the weight
before the lines began to run like watercolor.

**Expectation**

Twilight. No breeze. Humidity
condenses on my wine glass.
Air thickens, too, around the porch
as trees stand silent, waiting.
I sit alone, aware of news
and non-news, much the heavier load.

One friend is heavy with her own
expectancy at forty weeks:
knowing the what, but not the how,
the undeniable breaking forth,
intangible amid the crude
accessories of flesh and steel.

Another waits for test results
on a child who's ached and burned
since last year's tropic holiday.
Others sit vigil with the dying,
or with themselves, awaiting not
the sudden severing of light,
but more mundane catastrophes:
the cane, the dentures, hearing aids.

Thirty years ago tonight
and seven thousand miles away,
an army waited for the sign
to roll the tanks into the square.
What broke forth in Tiananmen
remains for history to tell
in whispers between videos,
the unofficial memories.

But here I sit, expecting only
mosquitoes with their thirsty mouths,
flutter of bats, and fireflies
that surely will light up the woods
beyond the windows' certain glare.

**Augury**

Today my friend awaits the doctor's call:
a reading of the cells that hold his fate.
I stand beside the bluff, scanning for signs.
Wet sandstone, golden in the fickle light,
turns dark as blood in shadow. On my left,
a mockingbird sings on the branch,
shifting its melody every few bars.
Over the valley, two hawks in counter-circles
swoop in and out of mist, then disappear.
The bird falls silent but still holds its perch.
Lacking the ancient art of augury,
I bend to pull a wet leaf from my shoe.
No, not a leaf. A feather. Holding it,
declaring it a sign, I turn toward home.

## Annunciation, March 2020

For eleven days already
we have kept ourselves
apart. We dare not even
break bread in church.

On your feast day, we honor
your flesh becoming Word,
the crumb of God in your belly.
The angel said, "Fear not."

But here, we feast on fear
of what may creep within us,
invisible, infectious.
We wash our knuckles red.

At dusk, a tornado warning.
I step outside to eerie calm,
the throb of treefrog song,
and (barely audible) a roar.

But soon the sirens scream.
The neighborhood contracts
as dangers magnify.
Whatever is revealed tonight

must be inside the cramped
closets and bathtubs where we crouch
with those we love, inhaling
each other's dubious breath.

**Enchantment**
*for my nephew, born during the pandemic*

Welcome to your crib,
safe and unenchanted
as a plain pine wardrobe
full of empty coats.
Your parents will lift you
to the spiny branches,
let you taste snow.
The fist outside your swaddle
grasps an invisible tale.

One day you'll touch
the soft place in the wall,
a seam with loosened threads.
You'll slip to a foreign shore
where strangely you are known.
You will protest the prophecies,
and mourn, "I'm not the one."
Even the lady with a torch
is not at liberty to put it down.

Break bread with the dragon,
dance with the wild things.
Somehow you'll know the hour
to ride home on a selkie's back.
Shaking off the foam and seaweed,
you'll find this world unmasked,
with lips and teeth discovered,
ears open as a shell
to hear the story only you can sing.

## Construction in the Neighborhood

Saw, drill, and hammer
    interrupt birdsong
        on this screened-porch afternoon.

Sometimes the crew
    dials in talk radio,
        country, or classic rock.

Bursts of machine sound
    join the canon of cicadas
        and woodpecker's staccato.

I'm just a guest—but aren't we all?
    —this screen a porous mask,
        a fragile web of presence.

Still, these are sounds of nesting, mating,
    saying, I'm here. Are you here too?
        Let's stay a while. Let's take

wood, iron, and clay, and build
    a space where we can touch
        within the wild, unfathomable world.

## Pandemic Questionnaire

*Have you experienced loss of smell or taste?*

No, but I can smell
sour worry on my breath,
stagnation in too many
days of undone laundry.

Yes, and I can taste
the bitter of stale coffee,
news pounding like a toothache,
the cheese gone slightly off.

But I can't even touch
my father in his bed.
Instead, I hold my phone:
a window on his room,

a screen where I appear
as ghostly as the figures
on his TV, or voices
bellowing from the hall.

And when I kill the screen
and take my eyes for a walk,
the smallest leaf or insect
can pin me where I stand,

listening to the songs
of wren and mourning dove.
When friends pass by, I wave,
palming the empty air.

## Fog Made of Stone

"What if the fog were made of stone?"
my son asked from the back seat
the week before the world shut down.
Practiced, I bounced the question back
like a tennis ball against a wall.
He answered, "We couldn't get through."
As tires gripped its slippery blur,
the road unwound into the mist.

"What if the stone were made of fog?"
—the question never asked that day
but implicit ever since,
everything that seemed solid
now porous as a sponge,
and bodies made of emptiness:
black boxes on a flat screen,
a needle's breadth between them.

And still, it's "Can you hear me?"
"Am I getting through?"
I think of Anticleia's shade
dissolving from Odysseus's embrace.
We hug the air instead of flesh
to keep the flesh unharmed.
If only this catabasis
brought prophecy to light.

## Laying out My Son's Clothes

I still lay out my son's clothes every night.
He doesn't need this management. He's eight,
and already resents my interference.
I make excuses, claiming it's to save
time in the morning, stress on my voice,
the endless repetition of *"Get dressed!"*

—which is to say, Armor yourself against
the world, which already knows your nakedness;
the lies that lurk behind a trusted face;
the pathogens that slip between the seams
of masks, and haunt the margins of our dreams;
the bruised fruit that can never be untasted.

## After a Dream of the End of Spring

What will spring mean, when winter melts
into the slush of memory—
a faded print: trees glazed with ice,
children bright-cheeked and bundled,
buffering in the snow?

What will spring mean, when water springs
beyond the banks, the walls we've built
to shore up scripture? Sea from dry land,
partition once was salutary,
or so we're told.

In the dream, I drove beside
a rising river black with blood.
What will spring from washed-out graves?
When seasons turn no longer,
where then will we go?

**Between Waves of the Pandemic**

A few, perhaps, heard rumbles.
The rest of us were caught
unawares, the first outsized drops
splattering like paintballs,
wind whipping trees like dervishes,
then sheets of rain shrouding the windows,
chimes clanging like a fire alarm.
Woe to those trapped outdoors.

And now, sun dapples the garden wall,
the leaves once more express themselves
in shadow. The arbor leaks, heavy and cool.
The bench invites, but it's too wet to stay.
All afternoon, the slow drip from the eaves.
Thunder again, like lions on the prowl.

**Why I Am Not Writing a Poem**

The cat sits in the window, looking out.
My throat is scratchy, sinuses athrob.
Geraniums dance in sunlight on the deck.
The washing machine upstairs shifts into spin.
I let my eyes unfocus, look at nothing.
The cat lies down across my writing arm.
A car passes the house, heading toward town.

**Gated Community**

Blueblack sky: the moon and stars still up.
No sound but the swoosh of sprinklers, feeding
grass for the shadowy workers to tend by day.
For now, the streets (with names like Hidden Heights,
Green Glades) belong to pasty-legged joggers,
the sidewalks to pedestrians and their dogs,
stepping around the mines of morning papers
and lakes and rivulets from watered lawns.
Dark woods speak mystery behind the houses,
an unnamed outer dark beyond the gates.
But here, now, in the indiscriminate lines
of landscape, a facsimile of peace
as starlight fades to birdsong-riddled morning
and muffled car horns punctuate the news.

## Dead Air

> *Steve Inskeep interviews a Chinese-American woman whose husband, a doctoral student in Persian history, is mysteriously detained in Iran.*

Three hundred marks on the wall,
hieroglyphs of hopeless time.
One daily hour of natural light,

a tricolored flag shadowing
the high-walled concrete yard.
The prisoners pace in circles, losing count.

Even when the phone line is pristine,
her loved one is a million miles away,
vanished, detained, forced to confess.

He cannot make a sentence,
cannot pronounce his sentence,
its duration twice his young son's age.

The reporter asks the not-quite-widow,
"What was his voice like?"
allowing dead air

to hang like the delay
in a lagging phone connection.
"He cannot make a sentence,"

she says. "He was just crying."
For a costly moment, the reporter
lets her silence be his silence,

and listening in my car,
I hold my breath,
their tears, our silences.

**Forty Trochees**

Have you found her
I don't know you
Hitting grounders
Let me show you

Children sleeping
Carry water
Someone's weeping
Here's your daughter

Put your shoes on
It's my birthday
Mass confusion
Shorter workday

Horseshoe tossing
Melanoma
Border crossing
Sweet aroma

Poet's market
Oxymoron
Drive or park it
There's a war on

**Physical**

My doctor shines a light into my ears
and sees a waxen tyrant's words congeal.

My doctor hears my alveoli tweet
the latest deals on Amazon and Etsy.

My doctor finds inside my nose the scent
of human traffic, sweatshops, pepper spray.

My doctor's stethoscope against my chest
hears bullets puncturing a classroom door.

My doctor has me read a foggy chart,
the letters melting faster than the ice.

My doctor says my reflexes are slow
to kick a leering bully in the groin.

My doctor looks between my legs and finds
a garden of contaminated fruit.

My doctor draws some blood and says, *You're fine.*

## Patient Belonging Bag

It's purely practical, of course.
Heavy-duty plastic, clear,
with a blank box for your name
—at best, an unconvincing link
to what's been shucked, an outer skin
of clothing, shoes, wallet, phone,
and jewelry. Things to be named
"effects" if someone else
is called to claim them.
Artifacts of who you were
before the heart attack,
the accident, the lump.

But what if it were, instead,
a bag of patient belonging?
A bag of tools: more rope, more slack,
more nerves when you are on your last.
Or else a space to crawl inside
and make yourself at home,
patient in all the fullness of that word,
suffering yourself to belong.

## You Have No Bucket

The man on the ground gasps, "I can't breathe."
The man on the cross rasps, "I thirst."
Like the soldiers standing by,
we numb ourselves
with the sour wine of vindication.

Jesus, as you hang thirsty on the cross,
do you recall the woman at the well
whom you asked for a drink?
It was hot that day. Sticky with dust,
her Samaritan clothes as damp as yours,
she questioned your question, knowing the custom
did not allow those who shared thirst
to share the quenching of it.
And then your parched throat spoke to her
of living water, inexhaustible.
"You have no bucket, and the well is deep,"
she said—but left her water jar behind,
running to tell the news.

The well is deep, so deep,
yet even in the desert, God split the rock
and water flowed out.
Bitter tears spring from cracked pavement.
Let our hearts of stone be broken
to quench your thirst.

**Pentecost**

The images are tired.
Both sacred wind and fire
seem incongruous at best
to us, who've seen the worst
of power on display.
When virus-laden breath
rhymes perfectly with death,
how dare we even pray
for holy inspiration?
Our very respiration
is further compromised
by gas and pepper spray.
And if the rhyme of *dove*
with *love* is too predictable,
a world that's sterilized
of spirit is unbearable.

**Savanna**

Smell of damp char, clean burn,
scorched trunks. Saw palms

reach up with spiky fingers,
sharpened to black.

Young longleaf pine
stretches like a child on tiptoe.

Carnivorous flowers:
pink sundew, pitcher,

open blood-tinged mouths
to fresh-fired air.

Bayou water thick and still.
Red-winged blackbird trills

yes, we are here,
preserved by fire.

**And Then**

And then there are days
when the air is so mild,
the current so gentle,
it holds you, benevolent,
like a lover's hand on your back,
a child's trusting grasp.

It holds
the birthday candles,
the IV drip,
the pink slip,
the rogue cells,
the unmade bed,
the blackened eye.

It holds.
In this still moving,
everything is held.
It is weather, and more than weather.
And it is very good.

**Jennifer Davis Michael** grew up beside a lake in Auburn, Alabama. She attended Oxford as a Rhodes Scholar and holds a doctorate from Northwestern University. Since 1995 she has taught English literature, primarily British Romanticism, at the University of the South in Sewanee, Tennessee, where she earned her B.A. Her monograph *Blake and the City* was published by Bucknell University Press in 2006. *Let Me Let Go*, published in 2020 by Finishing Line Press, was also a finalist in the Comstock Writers' Group Chapbook Contest. Her poem "Forty Trochees" was selected by Rachel Hadas for the Frost Farm Prize in Metrical Poetry in 2020. She is married to Jim Pappas, an Episcopal priest, and they have a young son.

CPSIA information can be obtained
at www.ICGtesting.com
Printed in the USA
LVHW100006271222
735905LV00003B/439